The Star in the East

THE STAR IN THE EAST

A SERMON PREACHED IN THE PARISH CHURCH OF ST. JAMES, BRISTOL, ON SUNDAY, FEBRUARY 26, 1809, FOR THE BENEFIT OF THE "SOCIETY FOR MISSIONS TO AFRICA AND THE EAST." (ON THE AUTHOR'S RETURN FROM INDIA.)

BY THE

REV. CLAUDIUS BUCHANAN, D.D.

LATE VICE-PROVOST OF THE COLLEGE OF FORT-WILLIAM IN BENGAL, AND MEMBER OF THE ASIATIC SOCIETY.

CURIOSMITH

MINNEAPOLIS
2012

Published by Curiosmith.
P. O. Box 390293, Minneapolis, Minnesota, 55439.
Internet: curiosmith.com.
E-mail: shopkeeper@curiosmith.com.

The Outline of the Contents was added to this edition by the publisher.

Previously published in 1809.

Supplementary content and cover design:
Copyright © 2012 Charles J. Doe.

ISBN 9781935626541

OUTLINE OF THE CONTENTS

———◆◇◆———

INTRODUCTION - THE MANIFESTATION OF THE DEITY SHOULD BE DISTINGUISHED BY A SUITABLE GLORY. (PAGE 7)

I. EVIDENCES EXISTING IN THE EAST, OF THE *GENERAL TRUTH* OF THE CHRISTIAN RELIGION. (PAGE 11)
  1. Ancient writings of India, containing particulars of the *History* of Christ. (PAGE 12)
  2. Certain doctrines of the East, shadowing forth the peculiar *doctrines* of Christianity, and manifestly derived from a common origin. (PAGE 13)
     First, The doctrine of the Trinity. (PAGE 13)
     Secondly, The doctrine of the incarnation of the Deity. (PAGE 13)
     Thirdly, The doctrine atonement for sin, by the shedding of blood. (PAGE 14)
     Fourthly, The doctrine of the influence of the Spirit of God. (PAGE 14)
  3. The state of the *Jews* in the East, confirming the truth of ancient prophecy. (PAGE 16)
  4. The state of the *Syrian Christians* in the East, subsisting for many ages, a separate and distinct people in the midst of the corruption and idolatry of the heathen world. (PAGE 17)

II. EVIDENCES OF THE *DIVINE POWER* OF THE CHRISTIAN RELIGION, EXEMPLIFIED IN THE EAST. (PAGE 18)
  1. The consequence of sending the Bible to the East. (PAGE 19)
  2. What has been done independently of our exertions. (PAGE 26)

CONCLUSION - THE TIME FOR DIFFUSING OUR RELIGION IN THE EAST IS COME. (PAGE 32)
  1. The minds of good men seem every where to be impressed with the duty of making the attempt. (PAGE 32)
  2. The general contemplation of the prophecies. (PAGE 33)

(*Continued on the next page.*)

3. The Holy Scriptures are translating into various languages. (PAGE 34)
4. The commotion in the bands of infidelity against the work of God. (PAGE 34)
5. The revolution of nations, and "the signs of the times." (PAGE 35)

TESTIMONY OF THE OPERATION OF THE GRACE OF GOD, IN "RENEWING A RIGHT SPIRIT WITHIN US." (PAGE 41)

THE STAR IN THE EAST

A SERMON BY THE

REV. CLAUDIUS BUCHANAN, D.D.

For we have seen his star in the east, and are come to worship him.—MATTHEW 2:2.

When, in the fullness of time, the Son of God came down from heaven to take our nature upon him, many circumstances concurred to celebrate the event, and to render it an illustrious epoch in the history of the world. It pleased the divine wisdom, that the manifestation of the deity should be distinguished by a suitable glory; and this was done by the ministry of Angels, by the ministry of Men, and by the ministry of Nature herself.

First, This was done by the ministry of *Angels;* for an Angel announced to the shepherds "the glad tidings of great joy which should be to all people;" and a multitude of the heavenly host sang "Glory to God in the highest, and on earth peace, good-will toward men."

Secondly, It was done by the ministry of *Men;* for illustrious persons, divinely directed, came from a far country, to offer gifts, and to do honor to the new-born King.

Thirdly, It was done by the ministry of *Nature*. Nature herself was commanded to bear witness to the presence of the God of Nature. A Star, or Divine Light, pointed out significantly from heaven the spot upon earth where the Savior was born.

Thus it pleased the Divine Wisdom, by an assemblage of heavenly testimonies, to glorify the incarnation of the Son of God.

All these testimonies were appropriate; but the *Journey* of the *Eastern Sages* had in it a peculiar fitness. We can hardly imagine a more natural mode of honoring the event than this, that illustrious persons should proceed from a far country to visit the child that was born Savior of the world. They came, as it were, in the name of the Gentiles, to acknowledge the heavenly gift, and to bear their testimony against that nation which neglected it. They came as the *representative*s of all the heathen; not only of the heathen in the East, but also of those in the West, from whom *we* are descended. In the name of the whole world, lying "in darkness, and in the shadow of death," they came inquiring for that Light which they had heard was to visit them in the fullness of time. "And the Star which they saw in the East went before them till it came and stood over where the young child was. And when they were come into the house, they fell down and worshipped him; and when they had opened their treasures, they presented unto him gifts, gold, and frankincense, and myrrh."

Do you ask how the Star of Christ was understood in

the East? or why Providence ordained that peculiar mode of intimation?

Christ was foretold in old prophecy, under the name of the "*Star* that should arise out of Jacob;" and the rise of the Star in Jacob was notified to the world by the appearance of an actual Star.

We learn from authentic Roman history, that there prevailed "in the East" a constant expectation of a Prince, who should arise out of Judea, and rule the world. That such an expectation did exist, has been confirmed by the ancient writings of India. Whence, then, arose this extraordinary expectation, for it was found also in the Sybilline books of Rome.

The Jewish expectation of the Messiah had pervaded the East long before the period of his appearance. The Jews are called by their own prophet the "Expecting people,"[1] (as it may be translated, and as some of the Jews of the East translate it) the "people looking for and expecting One to come." Wherever, then, the tribes of Israel were carried throughout the East, they carried with them their *expectation*. And they carried also the prophecies on which their expectation was founded. Now, one of the clearest of these prophecies runs in these words: "There shall come a *Star* out of Jacob."[2] And, as in the whole dispensation relating to the Messiah, there is a wonderful fitness between the words of prophecy and the person spoken of, so it was ordained, that the rise of the Star in

1 In Isaiah 18:2, "The people meted out," in our translation.
2 Numbers 24:17.

Jacob should be announced to the world by the appearance of an actual Star. A divine intimation of its nature and object, was, no doubt, given at the same time. And this actual Star, in itself a proper emblem of that "Light which was to lighten the Gentiles," conducted them to Him who was called in a figure the Star of Jacob, and the "glory of his people Israel."[3]

But again, why was the East thus honored? Why was the East, and not the West, the scene of these transactions?

The East was the scene of the first revelation of God. The fountains of inspiration were first opened in the East. And, after the flood, the first family of the new world was planted in the East. Besides, millions of the human race inhabit that portion of the globe. The chief population of the world is in those regions. And, in the middle of *them*, the Star of Christ first appeared. And, led by it, the wise men passed through many nations, tongues, and kindreds, before they arrived at Judea in the West; bearing tidings to the world that the Light was come, that the "Desire of all Nations" was come. Even to Jerusalem herself they brought the first intimation that her long-expected Messiah was come.

As the East had this honor in the first age of the Church, of pointing out the Messiah to the world; so now again, after a long interval of darkness, it is bearing witness to the truth of the religion of the Messiah; not indeed by the shining of a Star, but by exhibiting luminous evidence

---

3 The Jews used to speak of their Messiah under the appellation of *Bar Cocab*, or "the Son of the Star;" and false Christs actually assumed that name.

of the divine origin of the Christian Faith. It affords evidence of the general truth, not only of its *history*, but of its peculiar *doctrines;* and not of the truth of its doctrines merely, but of the *divine power* of these doctrines in convincing the understandings and converting the hearts of men. And in this sense it is, that "we have seen his Star in the East, and are come to worship him."

And when these evidences shall have been laid before you, you will see reason to think that the time is come for diffusing His religion throughout the world; you will "offer gifts" in His name for the promotion of the work; and you will offer up prayers in its behalf, "that God would be pleased to make his ways known upon earth, his saving health unto all nations."

In this discourse, we propose to lay before you,

1st, EVIDENCES existing in the East, of the *general truth* of the Christian Religion.

2nd, EVIDENCES of the *divine power* of that religion, exemplified in the East.

1. The *general truth* of the Christian Religion illustrated by certain evidences its the East. Of these we shall mention the following.

1. Ancient writings of India, containing particulars of the *History* of Christ.

2. Certain doctrines of the East, shadowing forth the peculiar *doctrines* of Christianity, and manifestly derived from a common origin.

3. The state of the *Jews* in the East, confirming the truth of Ancient prophecy.

4. The state of the *Syrian Christians* in the East, subsisting for many ages, a separate and distinct people in the midst of the heathen world.

These subjects, however, we must notice very briefly.

1. Hindoo history illustrates the *history* of the Gospel. There have lately been discovered in India certain Shanscrit writings, containing testimonies of Christ. They relate to a Prince who reigned about the period of the Christian era; and whose history, though mixed with fable, contains particulars which correspond, in a surprising manner, with the advent, birth, miracles, death, and resurrection of our Savior. Even supposing them to have been derived from the evangelical history, or spurious Gospels, it is remarkable, that they should have been recorded in the sacred language of the Brahmins, and incorporated with their mythology. The event mentioned in the Text is exactly recorded, namely, That certain holy men, directed by a Star, journeyed towards the West, where they beheld the incarnation of the Deity.[4]

These important records have been translated by a learned Orientalist[5] who has deposited the originals among the archives of the Asiatic Society. From these, and from other documents, he has compiled a work, entitled, "The History of the Introduction of the Christian Religion into India: its progress and decline." And,

4 This testimony of the *Hindoo* writer accords with that of the *Greek* writer *Chalcidius*, the ancient commentator on Plato, who adds, "that the infant Majesty being found, the wise men worshipped, and gave gifts suitable to so great a God." It is remarkable, that the History of the wise men, which is recorded by St. Matthew only, should be confirmed by Hindoos and Greeks.
5 Mr. Wilford.

at the Conclusion of the work, he thus expresses himself: "I have written this account of Christianity in India, with the impartiality of an Historian; fully persuaded that our holy religion cannot receive any additional luster from it."

2. There are certain *doctrines* of the East, shadowing forth the doctrines of Christianity.

The peculiar doctrines of the Christian Religion are so strongly represented in certain systems of the East, that we cannot doubt concerning the source whence these systems have been derived. We find in them the doctrines of the Trinity; of the Incarnation of the Deity, of the Atonement for Sin, and of the influence of the Divine Spirit.

First, The doctrine of the *Trinity*. The Hindoos believe in *one* God, Brahma, the creator of all things; and yet they represent him as subsisting in *three* persons; and they worship one or other of these persons throughout every part of India. And what proves that they hold this doctrine distinctly is, that their most ancient representation of the Deity is formed of one body and three faces. Nor are these representations confined in India alone; but they are to be found in other parts of the East.

Whence, then, my brethren, has been derived this idea of a TRIUNE God? If, as some allege, the doctrine of the Trinity among Christians be of recent origin, whence have the Hindoos derived it? When you shall have read all the volumes of Philosophy on the subject, you will not have obtained a satisfactory answer to this question.

Secondly, The doctrine of the *Incarnation* of the Deity. The Hindoos believe that one of the persons in their

Trinity (and that, too, the second person) was "manifested in the flesh." Hence their fables of the Avatars, or incarnations of Vishnoo. And this doctrine of the incarnation of the Deity is found over almost the whole of Asia.

Whence, then, originated this idea, that "God should become man, and take our nature upon him?" The Hindoos do not consider that it was an Angel merely that became man, but God himself. The incarnation of God is a frequent theme of their discourse. We cannot doubt whence this peculiar tenet of religion has been derived. We must believe that all the fabulous incarnations of the Eastern Mythology are derived from the real incarnation of the Son of God, or from the prophesies which went before it. Jesus the Messiah is the true AVATAR.

Thirdly, The doctrine of *Atonement* for Sin, by the shedding of blood. To this day, in Hindoostan, the people bring the Goat or Kid to the Temple, and the Priest sheds the blood of the innocent victim. Nor is this peculiar to Hindoostan. Throughout the whole East, the doctrine of a sacrifice for sin seems to exist in one form or other.

How is it then that some in this country say that there is no Atonement? For ever since "Abel offered unto God a more excellent sacrifice than Cain;" ever since Noah, the father of the new world, "offered burnt offerings on the Altar," sacrifices have been offered up in almost every nation; as if for a constant memorial before the world, that, "without shedding of blood, there is no remission of sin."

Fourthly, The doctrine of the influence of the *Spirit*

of God. In the most ancient writings of the Hindoos, some of which have been lately published, it is asserted that the "Divine Spirit, or light of holy knowledge," influences the minds of men. And the man who is the subject of such influence, is called "the man twice-born." Many chapters are devoted to the duties, character, and virtues of "the man twice-born."

If, then, in the very systems of the heathen world, this exalted idea should have a place, how much more might we expect to find it in the revelation of the true God; to which it must be traced?

We could illustrate other doctrines by similar analogies, did time permit. If these analogies were merely partial or accidental, they would be less important. But they are not casual; as must be known to every man who is versed in the Holy Scriptures and in Oriental Mythology. They are general and systematic. Was it ever alleged that the Light of Nature could teach such doctrines as these? They are all *beyond* the Light of Nature.

These, my brethren, are doctrines which exist in this day, in the midst of the idolatry and moral corruption of the heathen world. Every where there appears to be a *counterfeit* of the *true* doctrine. The inhabitants have lost sight of the only true God, and they apply these doctrines to their false gods. But these doctrines are relics of the first Faith of the earth. They are, as you see, the strong characters of God's primary revelation to man, which neither the power of man, nor time itself, hath been able to destroy; but which have endured from age to age, like the works of nature, the moon and stars, which God hath created incorruptible.

3. Another circumstance, illustrating the truth of the Christian religion in the East, is the state of the *Jews*. The Jews are scattered over the whole face of the East, and the fulfilment of the *prophecies* concerning them is far more evident in these regions, than it is here among Christian nations.

The last great punishment of the Jewish people was inflicted for their last great crime—their shedding the blood of the Son of God! And this instance of divine indignation has been exhibited to all nations; and all nations seem to have been employed by the appointment of God in inflicting the punishment.

By express prophecy, the Jews were sentenced to become "the scorn and reproach of people;" and "a proverb and bye-word among all nations." Now, that their stubborn unbelief should be a reproach to them amongst Christian nations here in the West, is not so strange; that they should be a proverb and a bye-word among those who had heard the prophecy concerning them, is not so remarkable. But to have seen them (as I have seen them) insulted and persecuted by the ignorant nations in the East; in the very words of prophecy, "trodden down of the heathen;" trodden down by a people who never heard the name of Christ; who never heard that the Jews had rejected Christ; and who, in fact, *punished the Jews without knowing their crime;* this, I say, hath appeared to me an awful completion of the divine sentence.

4. Another monument of the Christian religion in the East is the state of the *Syrian Christians;* subsisting, for many ages, a separate and distinct people, in the midst of the corruption and idolatry of the heathen world. They exist in the very midst of India, like the bush of Moses, burning and not consumed; surrounded by the enemies of their faith, and subject to their power, and yet not destroyed. There they exist, having the pure word of God in their hands, and speaking in their churches that same language which our Savior himself spake in the streets of Jerusalem.

We may contemplate the history of this people, existing so long in that dark region, as a type of the *inextinguishable Light* of Christ's religion; and, in this sense, it may be truly said, "We have seen his Star in the East."

The probable design of the Divine Providence, in preserving this people, appears to be this; That they should be a *seed* of the Church in Asia: that they should be a special instrument for the conversion of the surrounding heathen, when God's appointed time is come; a people prepared for his service, as fellow-laborers with us; a people, in short, in the midst of Asia, to whom we can point as an irrefragable evidence, of the truth and antiquity of the Christian Faith.[6]

6 The manuscripts in the Syriac language, which were found amongst the Syrian Christians, are now deposited in the public library of the University of Cambridge. They are twenty-five in number, and consist chiefly of copies of the Holy Scriptures, and of early Liturgies. The most important of them appears to be a copy of the Old and New Testament (without the Revelations) written on parchment, in large folio. It was presented to Dr. Buchanan by Mar Dionysius, the present Bishop of the *(Continued on the next page.)*

And this shall suffice as to the testimonies of the general truth of Christianity existing in the East.

II. We proposed, in the second branch of the discourse, to lay before you some evidences of the *divine power* of the Christian Religion exemplified in the East.

To say that Christianity has been propagated in the East, *as* other religions have been propagated, is to say little. It is little to say that thousands have adopted the *name*, and that it pervades populous provinces. For three centuries past, the Romish Church has diffused the *name* of Christianity throughout the East; and this success demonstrates how practicable it is to "propagate our religion" in the common sense of that expression. Providence seems to have ordained this previous labor of the Romish Church, to facilitate the preaching of the true gospel at the appointed time; for Christianity is found, even in its

---

Syrian Christians; (for Episcopacy has prevailed in every Christian region of the East from the first ages) and the tradition concerning it is, that it was given by the Patriarch of Antioch, of a former age, to his Indian Church. The words in this copy are all numbered. There is no date. But, from the character of some figures in it, a learned Antiquarian has conjectured, that it was written about the time of Charlemagne. Judging from the beauty of the writing, and from other circumstances, it is probable, that a later age will be finally assigned to it. Mr. Yeates, of Oxford, author of the Hebrew Grammar, is now employed in collating these Syriac MSS. as well as the other MSS. in the Hebrew and Ethiopic languages, brought by Dr. Buchanan from the East. Among the Hebrew MSS. is a roll of the Pentateuch, written on goat-skins, dyed red, upwards of forty-five feet long, which was found in one of the Synagogues of the black Jews in Hindoostan. It is remarkable, that this colony of Jews should live in a country adjoining to that or the Syrian Christians. There is one place, (the village of Chenotte, near Angamalee) where there is a Jewish Synagogue and a Christian Church. They stand over against each other; exhibiting, as it were, the LAW and the GOSPEL to the view of the heathen people.

worst form, to possess a moral and civilizing efficacy.

But it is in the East, as it is in the West—all are not Christians, who are called Christians. "He is not a Christian which is one outwardly; neither is that baptism which is outward in the flesh." The fact was this, the Romish Church preached Christianity in the East *without the Bible.*

Let us now enquire what has been the consequence of sending the Bible to the East. It is nearly one hundred years since the Bible was sent to the Hindoos; but not by our country. This honor belongs to the Protestant churches of Denmark and Germany. It was sent by them to the Tamulian nation, in the south of India; for there are many nations in Hindoostan. What then was the effect of giving them the Bible? It was the same as that which followed the giving the Bible to us, while we lay in almost Hindoo darkness, buried in the ignorance and superstition of the church of Rome. It gave light and knowledge; God blessed his own word to the conversion of the heart, and men began to worship him in sincerity and truth.

That province in India which was first blessed with the Bible, hath since continued to see "a great light." During nearly the whole of the last century, multitudes of Hindoos (both heathens and Roman Catholics) became members of the Protestant Church, one generation succeeding another; and amongst them there has ever been found, according to the records of their churches,[7] such a

---

7 These records are published in upwards of thirty volumes, thick 4to.

proportion, of serious piety, as you might expect to find, when the Gospel is preached with faithfulness and zeal.

During the whole of the last century, Providence favored them with a succession of holy and learned men, educated at the Universities of Germany; among whom was the venerable SWARTZ, called the Apostle of the East; and others not much inferior to him, men, whose names are scarcely known in this country, but who are as famous among the Hindoos, as Wickliffe and Luther are amongst us. The ministry of these good men was blessed in many provinces in the South of India, and the bounds of their churches are extending unto this day. The language of the country is called the *Tamul;* and the first translation of the Bible, in that language, was made, as we said, about a hundred years ago. Like Wickliffe's Bible with us, it became the parent of many versions, and, after a succession of improved editions, it is now considered by the Brahmins themselves, (like Luther's Bible in the German) as the classical standard of the Tamul tongue.

A Jubilee has lately been celebrated in India, in honor of the Gospel. In the month of July, 1806, a Jubilee was observed by these Hindoo churches, in commemoration of the arrival of the two first Protestant Missionaries on the 19th of July 1706. The year 1806, being the *hundredth* year (or the second fiftieth) since the Gospel first visited their land, was to them "the year of Jubilee." The happy occasion had been long anticipated, and was marked with demonstrations of joy and gladness; the people, as we were informed, walking in procession to their churches, carrying palms in their hands, and singing the 98th Psalm; and after offering up praises and thanksgiving to the Most High, they heard a sermon suitable to the day. The Sermon at the Jubilee of Tritchinopoly was preached by their aged Minister, the Rev. Mr. Pohle, from these words: "Go ye, therefore, and teach all nations; baptizing them in the name of the Father, and of the Son, and of the Holy Ghost."[8]

These were the effects of sending the Bible to the East. Men were "brought to the knowledge of the truth;" and at the end of a hundred years, the natives kept the Jubilee of the *Bible*.

Such, my brethren, was the Light in the South of India. And now a Light hath sprung up in the North, of which you have heard. Our own country hath begun, though late, to dispense "the word of Life." And although the time has been short, the success has been great. In the North, in the West, and in Ceylon, translations of the Scriptures are going on in almost all the languages of Oriental India. "In the fullness of time," we trust the different Christian societies of Britain have come forth, as with one consent, to commence the work of evangelizing the East. "In the fullness of time," hath this country begun, by these instruments, to employ her great power, and her enlightened zeal, in extending the knowledge of the true God throughout the world.

We ought not to regret that the work is carried on

---

8 See accounts of the "Society for promoting Christian Knowledge," for the year 1809.

by Christians of different denominations;[9] for if they teach the religion of the Bible, their labor will be blessed. We have no contentions in India, like those of Britain, between Protestants of different names. There they are all friends. The strife there is between Light and darkness; between the true God and an idol. So liberal is the Christian in Asia, (while he looks over the map of the World, and can scarcely find where the isle of Britain lies) that he considers even the term "Protestant" as being, in a certain degree, exclusive or sectarian. "The religion of the Bible," or, "the religion of Christ," is the name by which he would describe his creed. For, when the idolater once abjures his own cast for the Gospel, he considers the differences of Protestants (if he ever heard of them) as being very insignificant. Indeed he cannot well understand them. In the great revolution that takes place in his mind (if his conversion be real) he cannot contemplate these minute objects. We ought not then to regret that different classes of Christians are employed in the work. For the case is an exact parallel of that recorded in the Gospel: (Mark 9:38.) "And John answering said, Master, we saw one casting out Devils in thy name, and he followeth not *us;* and we forbad him, because he followeth not *us.* But Jesus said, FORBID HIM NOT."

---

9 The Protestant Missionaries in Bengal, who have been mentioned in terms of disrespect by some writers in England, are a respectable body of men, entitled to the support of their country, and are an honor to our Christian nation. The names of some of the humble *Teachers* of Christianity, will be remembered in India, when the *warriors* and statesmen of their age shall have been long forgotten.

On my arrival from India, a few months ago, I learned, that a controversy had engaged the attention of the public for some time, on the subject of sending Missions to the East. In the future history of our country it will scarcely be believed, that in the present age, an attempt should have been made to prevent the diffusion of the blessed principles of the Christian religion. It will not be believed, that books should have been written to prove, that it was wrong to make known the Revelation of the true God to our fellow-men; or that if, in some instances, it might be permitted, (as in the case of *remote* nations) yet that we ought not to instruct *that* people who were affirmed to be the *most* superstitious and *most* prejudiced; and who were also *our own* subjects. We scarcely believe ourselves that, twenty years ago, an attempt was made to defend the traffic in *slaves*, and that books were written to show, that this traffic was humane in its character, just in its principle, and honorable to our nation.

We trust, however, that the discussion which has taken place has been of important use. Men in general were not informed. The scene of action was remote, and the subject was new in almost all of its relations. Even to some of those persons, who had been in India, the subject was new. If you were to ask certain persons in his country, whether they had any acquaintance with *religious* families, they would answer, that "they did not know there *were* such families;"[10] so some from India hazarded an

10 Those families, who observe the daily worship of God in their houses, and by whom the name of God is never *(Continued on the next page.)*

opinion concerning what they called "the inveterate prejudices" of certain tribes in the East, who scarcely knew
the geography of the country where they lived; what their
religion was, or whether they had any religion at all. They
had seen no Star in the East; they had heard of no Jubilee
for the Bible. Like the spies of Israel, who brought back
"an evil report" from Canaan, they reported that India
was no "land of promise" for the Gospel; that the land
was *barren*, and that the men were *Anakims*. But the
faithful Swartz gave another testimony. He affirmed, that
it is "an exceeding good land;" and "his record is true."
He who was best qualified to give an opinion on the subject, who preached among the Hindoos for nearly fifty
years, founded churches among them in different provinces, established schools for their children, disseminated
religious tracts in their own tongue, and intimately knew
their language, manners, prejudices, and superstitions;
he who restored the Christian character to respect, after
it had fallen into contempt; he who was selected by the
natives as the arbiter of their differences with the English,
and whom both Hindoos and English loved and feared in
his life, and honored in his death;[11] this good man, I say,

mentioned but with reverence, are generally called *religious* families; to distin-
guish them from those who do *not* worship God, nor reverence his holy name.
11 At the funeral of Mr. Swartz, the Hindu Rajah of Tanjore came to do
Honor to his memory in the presence of his Brahminical court. *He covered
the body with a gold cloth, and shed a flood of tears.* He afterwards composed a
epitaph for him whom he called "his father and his friend," and caused it to
be inscribed on the stone which covers Swartz's grave, in one of the Christian
churches of Tanjore.

The English also pronounced a noble and affecting encomium on the
character of this estimable missionary. *(Continued on the next page.)*

differed widely in opinion from some, who have lately ventured to give a judgment in this matter: he affirmed, that it was England's DUTY to make known the Revelation of the true God to her Indian subjects.

In the mean time, while men hold different opinions on the subject here, the great work goes on in the East. The Christians there will probably never hear of our dissensions, nor, if they should hear of them, would they be much interested about them. And on this point I judge it right to notice a remarkable mistake, which appears to have existed on both sides of the question. It seems to have been assumed on the one side, and conceded on the other, that we have it in our power to prevent the progress of Christianity in India, if we should wish so to do; if such a measure were to be recommended by what is called "a wise policy." But we have *no* power to prevent the extension of the Christian religion in India. We have it in our power, indeed, greatly to *promote* it, but we have no power to *destroy* it. It would be as easy to extinguish Christianity

---

The honorable East-India Company have sent out to Madras a monument of marble, to be erected in the church of St. Mary at that place, to the memory of the Rev. Mr. Swartz, inscribed with a suitable epitaph; and they announced it in their general letter, dated the 29th of October, 1806, "as a testimony of the deep sense they entertained of his transcendent merit, of his unwearied labors in the cause of religion and piety; and of his public services at Tanjore, where the influence of his name and character was, for a long course of years, productive of important benefits to the Company." The Honorable Court further adds: "On no subject has the Court of Directors been more unanimous than in their anxious desire to perpetuate the memory of this eminent person, and *to excite in others an emulation of his great example.* "They direct finally, "that translations shall be made of the epitaph into the country languages, and published at Madras; and that the native inhabitants shall be encouraged to view the monument."

in Great Britain as in India. There are thousands of Christians in India—hundreds of thousands of Christians. And while we are contending here, whether it be a proper thing to convert the Hindoos, they will go on extending the bounds of their churches, keeping their Jubilees, and enjoying the blessings of the Gospel. While we are disputing here, whether the faith of Christ can save the heathens, the Gospel hath gone forth "for the healing of the nations." A congregation of Hindoos will assemble on the morning of the Sabbath, under the shade of a Banian tree, not one of whom, perhaps, ever heard of Great Britain, even by name. There the Holy Bible is opened; the word of Christ is preached with eloquence and zeal; the affections are excited; the voice of prayer and praise is lifted up; and He who hath promised his presence, "when two or three are gathered together in his name, is there in the midst of them to bless them," according to his word. These scenes I myself have witnessed; and it is in reference to them in particular I can say, "We have seen his Star in the East, and are come to worship him."

Thus far have we spoken of the success of the Gospel in Asia, by means of European preachers. But we shall now exhibit to you evidence from another source, from a new and unexpected quarter. We are now to declare what has been done, independently of *our* exertions, and in regions where we have no laborers, and no access. And this I do to show you, that whether we assist in the work or not, it is God's will *that it should begin.* You have hitherto been contemplating the Light in *India.* We are now to announce to you, that a Light hath appeared in *Arabia*, and dawned, as it were, on the Temple of Mecca itself.

Two Mahomedans of Arabia, persons of distinction in their own country, have been lately converted to the Christian faith. One of them has already suffered martyrdom. The other is now engaged in translating the Scriptures, and in concerting plans for the conversion of his countrymen. The name of the martyr is Abdallah;[12] and the name of the other, who is now translating the Scriptures, is Sabat: or, as he is called since his Christian baptism, Nathanael Sabat. Sabat resided in my house some time before I left India, and I had from his own mouth the chief part of the account which I shall now give to you. Some particulars I had from others. His conversion took place after the martyrdom of Abdallah, "to whose death he was consenting;" and he related the circumstances to me with many tears.

Abdallah and Sabat were intimate friends, and being young men of family in Arabia, they agreed to travel together, and to visit foreign countries. They were both zealous Mahometans. Sabat is son of Ibrahim Sabat, a noble family of the line of Bini-Sabat, who trace their pedigree to Mahomet. The two friends left Arabia, after paying their adorations at the tomb of their prophet, and travelled through Persia, and thence to Cabul. Abdallah was appointed to an office of state under Zemaun Shah, King of Cabul; and Sabat left him there, and proceeded on a tour through Tartary.

---

12 The word Abdallah is the same as Abdiel; and signifies the "Servant of God."

While Abdallah remained at Cabul, he was converted to the Christian faith by the perusal of a Bible (as is supposed) belonging to a Christian from Armenia, then residing at Cabul.[13] In the Mahometan states, it is death for a man of rank to become a Christian. Abdallah endeavored for a time to conceal his conversion; but finding it no longer possible, he determined to flee to some of the Christian churches near the Caspian Sea. He accordingly left Cabul in disguise, and had gained the great city of Bochara, in Tartary, when he was met in the streets of that city by his friend Sabat, who immediately recognized him. Sabat had heard of his conversion and flight, and was filled with indignation at his conduct. Abdallah knew his danger, and threw himself at the feet of Sabat. He confessed that he was a Christian, and implored him, by the sacred tie of their former friendship, to let him escape with his life. "But, Sir," said Sabat when relating the story himself, "I *had no pity*. I caused my servants to seize him, and I delivered him up to Morad Shah, king of Bochara. He was sentenced to die, and a herald went through the city of Bochara, announcing the time of his execution. An immense multitude attended, and the chief men of the city. I also went and stood near to Abdallah. He was offered his life if he would abjure Christ, the executioner standing by him with his sword in his hand. 'No,' said he, (as if the proposition were impossible to be complied with) 'I cannot abjure Christ.' Then one of his hands was

---

13 The Armenian Christians in Persia have among them a few copies of the Arabic Bible.

cut off at the wrist. He stood firm, his arm hanging by his side with but little motion. A physician, by desire of the king, offered to heal the wound if he would recant. He made no answer, but looked up steadfastly towards heaven, like Stephen, the first martyr, his eyes streaming with tears. He did not look with anger towards *me*. He looked at me, but it was benignly, and with the countenance of forgiveness. His other hand was then cut off. 'But, Sir,' said Sabat, in his imperfect English, 'he never *changed*, he never *changed*.' And when he bowed his head to receive the blow of death, all Bochara seemed to say, 'What new thing is this?'"

Sabat had indulged the hope, that Abdallah would have recanted, when he was offered his life; but, when he saw that his friend was dead, he resigned himself to grief and remorse. He travelled from place to place, seeking rest, and finding none. At last he thought that he would visit India. He accordingly came to Madras about five years ago. Soon after his arrival, he was appointed by the English government a Mufti, or expounder of Mahometan law; his great learning, and respectable station in his own country, rendering him well qualified for that office. And now the period of his own conversion drew near. While he was at Visagapatam, in the Northern Circars, exercising his professional duties, Providence brought in his way a New Testament in the Arabic language.[14] He read it with deep thought, the Koran lying

14 One of those copies sent to India by the "Society for Promoting Christian Knowledge."

before him. He compared them together with patience and solicitude, and at length the truth of the word of God fell on his mind, as he expressed it, like a flood of light. Soon afterwards he proceeded to Madras, a journey of 300 miles, to seek Christian baptism; and having made a public confession of his faith, he was baptized by the Rev. Dr. Kerr, in the English Church at that place, by the name of Nathanael, in the twenty-seventh year of his age.

Being now desirous to devote his future life to the glory of God, he resigned his secular employ, and came by invitation to Bengal, where he is now engaged in translating the Scriptures into the Persian language. This Work hath not hitherto been executed, for want of a translator of sufficient ability. The Persian is an important language in the East, being the general language of Western Asia, particularly among the higher classes, and is understood from Calcutta to Damascus. But the great work which occupies the attention of this noble Arabian, is the promulgation of the Gospel among his own countrymen; and from the present fluctuations of religious opinion in Arabia, he is sanguine in his hopes of success. His first work is entitled, (Neama Besharatin lil Arabi) *"Happy News for Arabia;"* written in the Nabuttee, or common dialect, of the country. It contains an eloquent and argumentative elucidation of the truth of the Gospel, with copious authorities admitted by the Mahometans themselves, and particularly by the Wahabians. And, prefixed to it, is an account of the conversion of the author, and an appeal to the well-known family in Arabia, for the truth of the facts.[15]

The following circumstance in the history of Sabat ought not to be omitted. When his family in Arabia had heard that he had followed the example of Abdallah, and become a Christian, they dispatched his brother to India (a voyage of two months) to assassinate him. While Sabat was sitting in his house at Visagapatam, his brother presented himself in the disguise of a saqueer, or beggar, having a dagger concealed under his mantle. He rushed on Sabat, and wounded him. But Sabat seized his arm, and his servants came to his assistance. He then recognized his brother! The assassin would have become the victim of public justice, but Sabat interceded for him, and sent him

---

15 Sabat is now at Dinapore, in Bengal, with the Rev. Mr. Martyn, Fellow of St. John's College, Cambridge, Chaplain to the East India Company, who is well qualified, by his knowledge of the Arabic and Persian languages, to superintend the labors of his companion. Mirza Fitrut, another celebrated Persian scholar, who visited England some years ago, and was afterwards employed in translating the Holy Scriptures in the College of Fort William, is engaged as the coadjutor of Sabat in his translation. Mr. Martyn himself is translating the Scriptures into the Hindoostanee language. In his latest letters, he speaks of his friend Sabat in terms of affection and admiration. Sabat accounted himself, at one time, the best mathematician and logician in Arabia. Mr. Martyn was senior Wrangler, or first mathematician of his year, at Cambridge, in 1801. In a letter, dated Sept. 1809, Mr. Martyn thus writes: "With my Arabian brother, and Mirza Fitrut, I am laboring most of the day in the Hindoostanee and Persian Gospels. The translation of the rest of the Holy Scriptures into these languages is employment enough for some years to come. At intervals I read Persian poetry, with Mirza, and the Koran with Sabat. These Orientals, with whom I translate, require me to point out the connection between every two sentences, which is often more than I can do. It is curious how accurately they observe all the rules of writing. Sabat, though a real Christian, has not lost a jot of his Arabian notions of superiority. He looks upon Europeans as mushroom, and seems to regard my pretensions to any learning, as we do those of a savage, or an ape."

home in peace, with letters and presents, to his mother's house in Arabia.

And these, my brethren, are the instances I wished to lay before you, of the divine power of the Christian religion recently exemplified in the East. The conversion of Abdallah and Sabat seems to have been as evidently produced by the Spirit of God, as any conversion in the primitive church, not accompanied with a sensible miracle. Other instances have occurred in Arabia of a similar kind, and on the very borders of Palestine itself. These are like the solitary notices which, in other nations, have announced the approach of general illumination.

You have now seen, 1. Evidences of the general truth of the Christian religion in the East; and, 2. Evidences of the divine power of that religion recently exemplified in the East. What conclusion, then, shall we draw from these facts? It is this: that the time for diffusing our religion in the East is COME.

We shall notice some other particulars which encourage us to think that the time is come.

1. The minds of good men seem every where to be impressed with the duty of making the attempt. Nearly fifteen years have elapsed since it began, and their ardor is not abated. On the contrary, they gather strength as they proceed; new instruments are found, and liberal contributions are made by the people. Indeed the consciences of men seem to bear witness that the work is of God.

The rapid success of this undertaking must appear almost incredible to those who are not acquainted with the fact. Translations of the Scriptures are carried on, not only in the languages of *India, Persia,* and *Arabia,* but in those also of *Burmah* and *China.* Mount *Caucasus,* in the interior of Asia, is another center of translation for the East, particularly for the numerous nations of the *Tartar* race. The Scriptures are preparing for the *Malayan* isles, and for the isles of the *Pacific* sea. The great continent of *Africa* has become the scene of different missions and translations. North and South *America* are sending forth the Scriptures. They are sent to the uttermost parts of the earth; to *Greenland, Labrador,* and *Austral Asia.* We might almost say, "There is no speech, nor language, where their voice is heard."[16]

And this spirit, for the diffusion of the truth, is not confined to Britain. It is found among good men of every Christian nation. Perhaps on this day prayers are offered up in behalf of the work, in Europe, Asia, Africa, and America. We are encouraged, then, to believe, that the time is come, in the first place, by the *consent* of *good men.* When I say good men, I mean religious and devout men, whose minds are not chiefly occupied with the politics and affairs of this world, but who are "looking for the consolation of Israel;" as it is expressed in these words, "Thy kingdom come."

2. Another circumstance, indicating that the time is at hand, is the general contemplation of the *prophecies.* The prophecies of Scripture are at this time pondered as

16 India, which solely occupies the minds of some persons in their discussion of the subject of missions, is but a *small part* of the nations which seek the word of God.

seriously in Asia, as in Europe. Even the Jews in the East begin to study the oracles of their prophet Isaiah. And, what is more important, the prophecies begin to be published among heathen nations; and we may expect, that every nation will soon be able to read the divine decree concerning itself.

3. The Holy Scriptures are translating into various languages.

When the Gospel was first to be preached to all nations, it was necessary to give a diversity of *tongues;* a *tongue* for each *nation;* and this was done by the Divine Power. But in this second promulgation, as it were, of the Gospel, the work will probably be carried on by a diversity of *translations,* a *translation* for each *nation.* Instead of the gift of tongues, God, by his Providence, is giving to mankind a gift of Scriptures.

4. Another circumstance, which seems to testify that the work is *of God,* is the commotion in the bands of infidelity *against it.* "Herod is troubled, and all Jerusalem with him." A spirit hath issued from the mouth of infidelity, which rageth against Him whose Star appeared in the East, and would destroy the work in its *infancy.* It rageth not against the Romish Church in the East, though that be Christian; nor against the Armenian Church in the East, though that be Christian; nor against the Greek Church in the East, though that be Christian; but it rageth against the religion of the Bible, that vital religion which aims at the conversion of the hearts of men.

Our Savior has said, "The Gospel shall be published

among all nations." But these resist the Divine Word, and say it cannot be published in all nations. Our Lord hath said, "Go ye into all the world, and preach the Gospel to every creature." But these allege, that the Gospel cannot be preached to every creature, for that "the bond of superstition is too strong, or that the influence of Christianity, is too weak."

These are unguarded words, and ought not to be heard in a Christian country. These are presumptuous words, arraigning the dispensation of the Most High. Such words as these were once spoken by the philosophers of Greece and Rome, but the Gospel prevailed, and first erected its dominion among *them*. In process of time the barbarous nations of Europe yielded to its dominion, of which *we* are evidences at this day. And the nations of Asia will yield to the same power, and the truth will prevail, and the Gospel shall be preached over the whole world.

5. The last circumstance which we shall mention, as indicating that the period is come for diffusing the Light of Revelation, is the *revolution of nations*, and "the signs of the times."

Men of serious minds, who are learned in the Holy Scriptures, and in the history of the world, look forward to great events. The judge of the future from the past. They have *seen* great events; events which, twenty years ago, would have appeared almost as improbable, as the *conversion of the whole world to Christianity*.

At no former period have the judgments of Heaven

been so evidently directed against the nations which are called Christian, as at this day. It is manifest, that God hath a controversy with his people, whatever be the cause. The *heathen* world enjoys a comparative tranquillity. But the *Christian* nations are visited, in quick succession, by his awful judgments. What, then, is the cause of the judgments of God on his Christian people? If we believe the declarations of God, in his Holy Word, we shall ascribe them to their rejecting, so generally, the TESTIMONY OF CHRIST. That nation which first "denied HIS name before men," was first given up to suffer terrible judgments itself, and is now permitted to become the instrument of inflicting judgments on others. And this is agreeable to the ordinary course of God's just and retributive Providence. That kingdom which first seduced others by its infidelity, is now become the instrument of their punishment.

The same retributive Providence is "making inquisition for the blood of the saints." The massacres, fires, and anathemas of a former day filled the minds of men with dismay. *We* forget these scenes, but all things are present with God. For a long time (as men count time) God kept silence; but the day of retribution is at length arrived, and the seats of the Inquisition must be purged with blood.

From the fury of these desolating judgments *we* have hitherto been preserved. "Righteousness exalteth a nation." (Proverbs 14:34.) It would appear as if God would thus do honor to a Church holding pure doctrine, and to a State, united with that Church, which hath defended the true Faith, from the superstitions and corruptions which have so long reigned in the Christian world. Lately, indeed, it should seem as if God had selected this nation, as he formerly did his chosen people Israel, to preserve among men a knowledge of the true religion; for we have been called to stand up, as it were "between the living and the dead," in defence of Christian principles. And although it be true that we have fought rather for our country than for our religion, yet it is also true that religion is, in present circumstances, identified, in a certain degree, with the existence of our country. And we trust, that it is in the purpose of Providence, by upholding the one, to save the other also.

Let this nation, then, weigh well what it is, in God's moral administration of the world, which preserves *her* at this period. Let her beware of infidelity, and of that moral *taint* which ever accompanies it. Is it true that any of our chief men begin to "laugh at vice," like Voltaire? Let us recall to view the experience of France. We beheld infidelity gradually infecting that nation, even as poison insinuates itself through the human frame, till the whole body of the great was contaminated. Then was their iniquity full, and God's judgment began. Now, though it be true, that the faith of our Church is pure, "that she holdeth the head," that she is founded on the Prophets, Evangelists, and Apostles; though it be true that there is in the midst of her a large body of righteous persons, men possessing sound learning, enlightened zeal, and pure charity; men who are called by our Savior, "the light of the world," and "the salt of the earth;" yet it is equally certain, that the greater part of her members are not of that description. It is certain, that the *spot* of moral disease has been long visible. And we know not whether the true state of the nation may not be this; that there is just "salt" enough (to use the figure of the Gospel) to preserve the body from corruption.

Let us then consider well what it is which, in the present circumstances of the world, saves this nation. If it be the divine pleasure, to save *us*, while other nations are destroyed, it cannot be on account of the *greatness of our empire*, or of our *dominion by sea*, or of our *extended commerce*. For why should the moral Governor of the world respect such circumstances as *these?* But if we are spared, it will be, we believe, on account of our MAINTAINING the pure religion of Christ as the RELIGION OF OUR LAND, and promoting the knowledge of that religion, and of the blessed principles which accompany it, throughout the rest of the WORLD. This may be a consideration worthy of the divine regard. Chiefly, on our being an instrument of GOOD to the world, must depend our hope of surviving the shocks and convulsions which are now rending in pieces the other nations of Europe.

We shall now recapitulate the evidences noticed in this discourse, which encourage us to believe, that the time is come for disseminating the knowledge of Christianity in the heathen world.

1. The facility with which Christianity is propagated generally in Asia, wherever the attempt has been made.

2. The peculiar success that has attended our own

THE STAR IN THE EAST

endeavors to promote the religion of the Bible.

3. The conversion of illustrious persons in Asia, by means of the Bible alone.

4. The translation of the Bible into almost all the languages of Asia; promising, as it were, a second promulgation of Christianity in the East.

5. The general contemplation of the prophecies in Europe and Asia.

6. The general commotion among the bands of Infidelity, who are hostile to the design, both in Europe and Asia.

7. The consent of good men, in all Christian nations, to promote the design. And,

8. The preservation of our own country, to carry on the work, amidst the ruin or infidelity of other nations. To which may be added,

9. The subjugation of so large a portion of Asia to the British dominion.

Behold, then, my brethren, the great undertaking, for the promotion of which you are now assembled. If it were in the power of this assembly to diffuse the blessings of religion over the whole world, would it not be done? Would not all nations be blessed? You perceive that some take a lively interest in this subject, while others are less concerned. What is the reason of this difference? It is this: Every man, who hath felt the influence of religion on his own heart, will desire to extend the blessing to the rest of mankind; whereas, he who hath lived without concern about religion, will not be solicitous to communicate to others a gift which he values not himself. At the same time, perhaps, he is not willing to be thought hostile to the work. But there is no *neutrality* here. "He that is not with Christ," in maintaining his kingdom on earth, "is against Him." And so it appeareth to God, "who searcheth the heart." Every one of us is now acting a part in regard to this matter, for which he must give an account hereafter. There is no one, however peculiar he may reckon his situation or circumstances, who is exempted from this responsibility. For this is the criterion of obedience in the sight of God, even our conduct in receiving or rejecting the "record which God hath given of his Son." And no man "receiveth this record" in sincerity and truth, who will not desire to make it known to others. You have heard of the conversion of Mahometans and Hindoos. Yes, our Lord hath said, "Many shall come from the East and from the West, and shall sit down with Abraham, and Isaac, and Jacob, in the kingdom of Heaven; but the children of the kingdom shall be cast out."

Begin, then, at this time, the solemn inquiry, not merely into the general truth of Christ's religion, but into its divine and converting power. You observe, that in this discourse I have distinguished between the *name* of Christianity, and the *thing*. For it seems, there are some who having departed from the ancient principles of our reformation, admit the *existence* of the Spirit of God, yet deny his *influence;* who agree not with the Apostle Paul, that the "Gospel cometh not in *word* only," but "in *power*, and in the Holy Ghost, and in much assurance."

Begin, then, the important inquiry; for "the time is short," and this question will soon be brought to issue before an assembled world. In the mean time I shall offer to you my testimony on this subject.

The operation of the grace of God, in "renewing a right spirit within us," (Psalm 51) is a doctrine professed by the whole faithful Church of Christ militant here on earth. The great Author of our religion hath himself delivered the doctrine, in the most solemn manner, to the world. "Verily, verily, I say unto you, Except a man be born again, he cannot see the kingdom of God." *Verily, verily;* it is an undoubted truth, an unchangeable principle of the heavenly dispensation, that except a man be renewed in his mind by the Spirit of God, he shall not have power even to *see* or behold the kingdom of God. What though many in our day deny this doctrine? A whole nation denied a doctrine, greater if possible than this. The very name and religion of Christ have been denied in our time. But if our Savior hath delivered any one doctrine of the Gospel more clearly than another, it is this of a spiritual conversion; and the demonstration of its truth is found in all lands, where his Gospel is known. Christians, differing in almost every thing else, are agreed in this. Differing in language, customs, color, and country; differing in forms of worship and church government, in external rites and internal order; they yet agree in the doctrine of a change of heart, through faith in Christ; for this hath been the grand characteristic of Christ's religion among all nations, tongues, and kindreds, where the Gospel hath been preached, through all ages down to this day. This is, in fact, that which distinguishes the religion of God in Asia from the religions of *men*. In every part of the earth, where I, myself, have been, this doctrine is proclaimed, as the hope of the sinner and the glory of the Savior. And again, in every place it is opposed, in a greater or less degree, by the same evil passions of the human heart. In rude nations, the same arguments are brought against it, in substance, which are used here in a learned country. Among ignorant nations a term of reproach is attached to serious piety, even as it is here among a refined people; thereby proving what our Lord hath taught, that the superior goodness inculcated by his Gospel would not be agreeable to all men; and that some would revile and speak evil of his disciples, "for righteousness sake;" thereby proving what the Apostle Paul hath taught, that "the Cross of Christ is an offence" to the natural pride of the human heart; that "the carnal mind is enmity against God;" and that "the natural man receiveth not the things of the Spirit of God, because they are spiritually discerned."[17]

17 The late learned and judicious PALEY has given his dying testimony to the truth of this doctrine. (See his Sermons, p. 119.) "A change so entire, so deep, so important as this, I do allow to be a CONVERSION; (he had said before, 'there must be a revolution of principle; there must be a revolution within;') and no one who is in the situation above described *can be saved* without undergoing it; and he must necessarily both be sensible of it at the time, and remember it all his life afterwards. It is too momentous an event ever to be forgot. A man might as easily forget his escape from shipwreck. Whether it was sudden, or whether it was gradual, if it was effected (and the fruits will prove that,) it was a *true conversion;* and every such person may justly both believe and say it himself, that he was converted at a particular assignable time."

Paley here speaks the language of the true Church of Christ, in all ages and nations.

I have thought it right, my brethren, to deliver to you my testimony at this time; to assure you that the Gospel which begins to enlighten the East, is not "another Gospel," as the Apostle speaks, but the same as your own. There is one Sun; there is one Gospel. "There is one Lord, one Faith, one Baptism;" and there is one JUDGEMENT. May we be all prepared to give our answer on that day!

You are now invited to contribute some aid towards the extension of the religion of Christ. You are now, to present "your gifts" before Him who was born Savior of the world; and to send back those "glad tidings" to the East, which the East once sent to you, namely, that the Light is come, that "the Desire of all nations is come." Let every one who prays with his lips, "Thy kingdom come," prove to himself, his own sincerity, that he really desires in his heart that the kingdom of Christ should come. Blessed is the man who accounts it not only a duty, but a privilege, to dispense "the word of life." It is, indeed, a privilege, and so you will account it hereafter, when you shall behold all nations assembled before the judgment-seat of Christ. If you be then numbered with his people, you will reflect with joy that you were enabled, at this time, "to confess His name before men," and to afford some aid for the "increase of his government," and of his glory upon earth. And let every one who lends his aid accompany it with a prayer, that the act may be blessed to himself, in awakening his own mind more fully to the unutterable importance of the everlasting Gospel.

NOTES

NOTES

MAN'S QUESTIONS & GOD'S ANSWERS

Am I accountable to God?
"Every one of us shall give account of himself to God." (Romans 14:12).

Has God seen all my ways?
"All things are naked and opened unto the eyes of Him with whom we have to do." (Hebrews 4:13).

Does He charge me with sin?
"The Scripture hath concluded all under sin." (Galatians 3:22).
"All have sinned." (Romans 3:23).

Will He punish sin?
"The soul that sinneth, it shall die." (Ezekiel 18:4).
"For the wages of sin is death." (Romans 6:23).

Must I perish?
"God is not willing that any perish, but that all should come to repentance." (2 Peter 3:9).

How can I escape?
"Believe on the Lord Jesus Christ, and thou shalt be saved." (Acts 16:31).

Is He able to save me?
"He is able also to save them to the uttermost that come unto God by Him." (Hebrews 7:25).

Is He willing?
"Christ Jesus came into the world to save sinners." (1 Timothy 1:15).

Am I saved on believing?
"He that believeth on the Son hath everlasting life." (John 3:36).

Can I be saved now?
"Now is the accepted time; behold, now is the day of salvation." (2 Corinthians 6:2).

As I am?
"Him that cometh to Me I will in no wise cast out." (John 6:37).

Shall I not fall away?
"Him that is able to keep you from falling." (Jude 24).

If saved, how should I live?
"They which live should not henceforth live unto themselves, but unto Him which died for them." (2 Corinthians 5:15).

What about death, and eternity?
"I go to prepare a place for you; that where I am, there ye may be also." (John 14:2, 3).